DEDICATION

TO ALL OF MY GRANDKIDS, ESPECIALLY MISS KENNIDY.

WITHOUT WHOM, THIS STORY WOULD JUST BE LOST

IN MEMORY AND NOT SHARED ON THESE PAGES.

YOU ALL HAVE PROVEN TO ME THAT THE YOUNGEST

AMONG US CAN HAVE THE VERY BEST IDEAS, BRIGHTEST

ATTITUDES AND BIGGEST HEARTS.

LOVE YOU ALL!

GRANDMA SANDIE

My Day With Mabel (Sammy's Story)

Six year old Sammy, a curious little girl with sparkles in her eyes, was traveling with her mom one morning to get her hair cut. When all of a sudden her Mom said ,

"There's something in the road up ahead!" and struggled to see what it could be as she slowly approached.

Sammy sat up in her booster seat and stretched as tall as she could to try to see out the window to the road ahead and get a glimpse of what her Mom was seeing.

"Oh my!" Said Sammy's Mom with alarm, "It seems to be moving."

Now Sammy could hardly stand the suspense! With excitement she asked

"What? What is it? What is it doing? What IS it, What could it be?"

As their car slowly approached the now squirming object, Sammy's Mom was starting to figure out what the object ahead of them was, and her face started to look saddened.

Sammy's eyes grew large as she saw her Mom's expression turn to a troubled look.

"Mommy! What is it?", Sammy demanded with growing concern.

Sammy's Mom finally brought the car to a stop where she and Sammy both jumped out of the car and carefully walked up to the front of the car to see what this mysterious object was that was lying on this road next to a large pond.

There, in the road, a squirming and frightened greyish, yellowish, and fuzzy baby Canadian Goose was laying on it's side, unable to get up due to an injury of some sort.

After seeing that the baby goose couldn't get up on it's own, Sammy's Mom helped the baby goose get on it's feet again. The little goose wobbled in a dizzying circle, staggered and stumbled before falling to it's side again in exhaustion. Sammy's Mom concluded that this baby goose must have been hit by a car or truck.

Sammy knelt down on the ground next to the fuzzy flailing creature and gently stroked it's long neck. The baby goose seemed to relax with Sammy's tender and soothing touch.

Sammy whispered softly to her new friend.

"It's okay, I'll take care of you." And at that very moment she made a decision and she whispered, "I will name you Mabel".

Sammy turned to look up at her Mom, who had one little tear glistening on her cheek as she watched Sammy treat this injured Baby with such tenderness. Sammy's Mom said to her little girl.

"Well honey, we are going to be late so we better get going." as she turned to walk away from the scene.

Sammy jumped to her feet and quickly ran around to the front of her Mom, blocking her from walking further. With a shaking voice and a quivering chin, Sammy pleaded,

"Mommy ! No! We can't leave her here. We have to take her with us! We must help her get better! Please Mommy! Please!"

Sammy's Mom quickly realized that Sammy was not going to give this up. So, with defeat in her voice, she finally said,

"Okay Sammy. We'll take the Baby goose with us and we will try to nurse her back to health. But…" As she held up her hand "Once she is better, we will bring her back here to this pond to find her family again." Then she added as an after thought, "But you are going to take care of her, and clean up after her until we can bring her back here. Do you understand?"

"Yes! Yes Mommy!" Sammy said with enthusiasm, "I promise I will take real good care of Mabel!"

With that, Sammy returned to the injured goose and gently scooped Mabel up into her arms and Mabel seemed to understand. She responded to Sammy's tender embrace with a weak little "Weep weep weep."

Mabel stayed warm and secure in Sammy's arms as they drove on to get their haircuts. Mabel stretched her graceful long neck up to rest her chin on Sammy's shoulder. Sammy whispered encouraging words to Mabel and Mabel whispered back "Weep Weep Weep".

When Sammy and her Mom arrived at the hair salon, they knew they couldn't leave Mabel alone in the car, so

Sammy carried Mabel into the salon where all of the ladies getting their hair done turned and gasped at this little girl carrying a wild baby goose. But by this time, Mabel seemed pretty comfortable in the warm embrace of Sammy's arms. She looked around at everybody staring at her, and hid her face under Sammy's pigtailed hair.

Sammy's Mom explained how they found Mabel and all the ladies understood how this scene came to be.

The nice salon owner brought out a good sized box lined with towels for Sammy to set Mabel into. Sammy bent over to put Mabel into the box and Mabel settled into the box with a quiet little "Weep weep weep".

After their hair cuts were done, Sammy and her Mom brought Mabel to their house where Sammy prepared a nice little enclosure with lots of long grass that Sammy had picked and a large pan of water. But something was different with Mabel. She

still had her little "weep weep weep" but all of a sudden she was able to stand on her own.

Sammy sat for hours inside the small enclosure and talked to Mabel. Mabel walked around, nibbled on the grass and drank the water in between her "weep weep weeps".

[14]

Then she came over and rested in the crook of Sammy's leg and took a little nap. Sammy fell asleep for a while too.

When Mabel awoke, she jumped to her feet which startled Sammy awake as well.

Sammy ran her hands down Mabel's graceful long neck, then over the rest of her downy body, trying to see if Mabel had any areas that seemed like they hurt. Mabel did not seem to mind at all, but also didn't seem to have any injuries. She seemed just fine. Her "weep weep weeps" were a little stronger. And she also seemed a little spunky.

Sammy had been talking to Mabel all afternoon in her enclosure, so Mabel did not act surprise as Sammy said to her,

"It's really hard to believe that after just a few hours, I already love you Mabel. You are so sweet and I am so glad that you are feeling better." Then as tears sprung from her eyes, Sammy knew what she had to do. She knew that it was the right thing to do, but also knew that it was going to be so hard .

Sammy's Mom quietly walked in to the garage where Sammy and Mabel were and she heard what Sammy had said to Mabel. She felt a lump in her throat as she realized her little girl was crying.

"Sammy..." she said with deep concern "What is wrong? Why are you crying? Is Mabel hurt worse than we thought? Or...." She paused as she gently wiped a tear from Sammy's face. "Tell me what is wrong Dear."

By then Sammy was trying as hard as she could to hold back a sob, but what she said next confused her Mom a little.

"Mabel seems to be all better. Look at her Mom!" Sammy said, She's walking! She's eating! She doesn't seem hurt at all!" As a sob slipped out with her words.

Sammy's Mom tilted her head and looked at her daughter and said,

"I don't understand. Why does that make you cry?"

Sammy took a deep breath and gathered all her strength and will.

"Mom! We must take her back to the pond. Where we found her, so that she can be with her family!" She was still crying as she said "It's the right thing to do!" Then

Sammy threw herself into the arms of her Mom as she cried…. "I just love her so much and I'm glad she's better, but I'm going to miss her SO MUCH!"

Sammy's Mom stroked her little girls head, comforting her in her arms. She knew that was a hard decision for her daughter to make, but she was so proud of her little girl for making it.

Sammy's Mom reminded her that sometimes doing the right thing is not always easy thing. But bringing Mabel back to her family will probably make Mabel very happy and that is what was important.

Together, they gathered Mabel up into Sammy's arms once again, and got back in the car to head to the spot where they

had found Sammy's newest friend. Mabel cuddled her head into Sammy's neck with a little "Weep weep weep."

[21]

It had been raining when they left the house with Mabel and they were a bit worried that there would be too much rain for them to set Mabel free.

When they arrived at the spot where they had first found Mabel, The rain had stopped and Sammy's Mom pulled the car over to the side of the road closest to the pond. She looked at her daughter to let her know it was time.

Sammy took a deep breath and swallowed hard, then they all got out of the car. Sammy was still carrying Mabel as she walked to the edge of the pond. Mabel hid her head under Sammy's hair but Sammy and her Mom noticed that across the pond there was two adult geese and three smaller ones that looked just the same age as Mabel.

Sammy gave Mabel one last hug, and a kiss on the top of her downy head then set her in the water at the edge of the pond. Mabel quickly began to swim like an expert, then she stopped. She circled back around to where Sammy stood, looked her in the eye and let out a "weep weep weep."

[24]

Then turned once more to head out to the open pond. By then the two adult geese on the other side had seen what was going on and had entered the water to begin swimming toward Mabel followed by all three of the youngsters. Then, one of the adult geese swam ahead of the group and got closer and closer to Mabel. Sammy and her Mom could hear Mabel's "weep weep weep" and the adult goose approached Mabel and also said "Weep Weep Weep", Touched the tip of it's beak to Mabel's beak then made a circle around Mabel and ushered her back to her family where they all seemed so happy to be reunited.

Both Sammy and her Mom had happy tears running down their cheeks as they watched the two adult geese and four goslings swim together in a group, and all were singing the same song. "Weep Weep Weep."

Just before they turned to walk back to the car, a rainbow appeared in the sky over the family of geese as they swam.

Sammy turned to her Mom and said

"Thank you Mommy! I'll never forget my day with Mabel"